The Rise ABOVE the Clouds

Kayvonna K. Stigall

The Rise Above the Clouds
Copyright © 2016 Kayvonna K. Stigall

All rights reserved. No part of this book may be reproduced or transmitted in any form or by any means, electronic or mechanical, including photocopying, recording or by any information storage and retrieval system, without permission in writing from the publisher.

Cover Design: Creativelogoart
Cover Photo: TrilogyBeats313
Personal Photo: Da'Vis Images
Editing: So It Is Written, LLC

ISBN: 978-1-937400-63-7

Printed in the United States of America

Published by Manifold Grace Publishing House, LLC
Southfield, Michigan 48033
www.manifoldgracepublishinghouse.com

Dedication

In loving memory of my mother,

Juanita Tolbert-Sellers

"Granny – you can do whatever you want as long as you keep God first and work hard."

I'll see you when I get there.

Acknowledgments

First and foremost I would like to thank God who is the head of my life!

I would like to thank my husband Karl who has been on this journey called life with me for 16 years so far! I love you and I know the best is yet to come for our family!

Also, special thanks to...

My Aunt Patricia Eady who has always been more like a second mom to me...I love you.

My cousins Kembria Barnes and Nathayai Washington, you both are like my older sisters and two of the strongest women I know, thanks for always being there for me...3 amigas for life!.

Janice McCarter who has spoken life in my ear on many occasions when I wanted to throw in the towel.

My Pastor Daniel R. Grandberry and my First Lady Sis. Jeannine Grandberry who have been a great example to me on so many different levels....I love you both.

Contents

Dedication	v
Acknowledgment	vii
The Beginning, The Middle and the End	1
My Savior's Eyes	3
This Kind	4
I Lie Awake	5
Jesus You're Everything	6
In the Press	7
She Played It Out (A Tribute to Maya Angelou)	8
Just Me! (Who Said That Wasn't Enough?)	10
When I Thought	14
Really	16
R.I.P. Flesh	17
The Perfect Love Story	19
See It Before You See It	20
Failure's Not an Option	21
Letter (or Notice) to the Devil	22
Stop Being So Selfish	24
Don't Stop Praying	26
Pounding Heart	27

The Main Thing	29
Beauty	30
Say Whaaat?	32
You See	33
What's Next?	34
Devil, You Make Me Sick!	35
Get the Truth	36
Just My Rant	38
Pray for My Generation	39
I'm Already Convinced	41
About the Author	43

The Beginning, The Middle and The End

Spirit of Heaviness

A spirit of heaviness, lining the soul with sorrow and anguish. God's warm everlasting love can coat and penetrate the hardest of hearts and break through the concrete walls of despair. How can we expect Him to *NOT* love? He lays out the plan. All we have to do is follow. Thank you Jesus for *FORGIVENESS*!

The Love We Should Know

The love we should know is the love that has always been in the hearts of the kind words of the light of day. The love in the morning breath we breathe, which allows us to pulsate uncontrollably, *NOT* by our own will, but by the grace we've been given to wake up and say, "Good morning! Thank you, Jesus, for your love!"

The Skin I'm In

I'm happy in the skin I'm in! But oh so overjoyed that when this flesh of beige

PIGMENT BEGINS TO SHOW THE WRINKLES OF THIS LIFE, I WILL NOT BE LEFT IN IT TO SUFFER THE DESTINY OF DECOMPOSITION. I SHALL BE LIKE THAT OF AIR. FREE. BREATHING THE BREATHABLE, MORE ALIVE THAN ALIVE. THE NEWEST THAT NEW CAN BE! THANK YOU, JESUS, FOR FREEDOM!

My Savior's Eyes

As I kneel and cry, I wonder who wipes our Savior's eyes?
Surely the world's malice and destruction
Grieves His spirit because it's against His instruction.
I wonder. My, my, my! Who wipes our Savior's eyes?
As the world seeks out people and things to fill His place,
or any tangible thing to put a smile on their face.
I look to the sky. Who wipes our Savior's eyes?
Love of money trumps respect and industry power causes self-worth neglect.
Do you wonder like I? Who wipes our Savior's eyes?
Family against family, unconditional love out the door.
Hearts pulsating from being stepped on because only His blood can restore.
Can I get a tweet, status update or reply? Who wipes our Savior's eyes?
How do we do it? How do we make the tears vaporize?
By *living through* our Savior's eyes!

This Kind

Life stands still when your name is spoken.
Though the ocean runs deep to a dark bottomless end,
Yet and still, my love surpasses its profundity in weight.
This "kind" has to come with a price,
A price that sure cannot be compensated with trivial earthly exchange.
This "kind" provokes rage and humbleness,
Trials and triumphs,
Insecurities and assurance.
It cannot be bound by the mountains and valleys of everyday circumstance.
It will not bow down to the ordinary.
Oh, the wretch it has made me at times.
Yet the fiery ocean tides have washed away
The impurities of mistrust and conflict.
And refined me into a more polished and elated soul.
The journey has been long, but worth it all.
Joy has taken over the happy, which needed something to "happen" to exist.
The joy is here, no matter how the season may transform.
Joy can travel to the pits of hell to retrieve my love,
And redeem its weight without time passing by.
It can reach down to the inner-most parts of the earth,
Where my human eyes are constrained,
And convey the assurance of my commitment to my love
In places where there
Is doubt,
This "kind" is worth it.

I Lie Awake

I lie awake, although my eyes are closed,
Drowning out the sound of cries
With my tears and disbelief.
I lie awake, although my eyes are closed,
Shivering from realities
And troubles of this world.
I lie awake, although my eyes are closed,
Praying for the Comforter
And all His promises.
I lie awake, although my eyes are closed,
Putting on the Whole Armor,
Though behind the breastplate
Of righteousness lies my quivering flesh.
I lie awake, although my eyes are closed.
No wavering faith…I believe!
But help me with my unbelief.

Jesus, You're Everything

Jesus, you're everything!
Jesus, you're everything!
You are my breath.
You're more than more to me,
Stronger than strong to me.
You are my everything!
You are my breath.
You're greater than great to me,
Much more than this world could ever be.
You are my everything!
You are my breath!

In the Press

The road to salvation may get lonely,
And at times you may stumble off the path.
But one thing that remains constant and strong,
Is the love God has.
So when the trials have overtaken your strength,
And you've finally surrendered,
Know that that's when God can take over.
So push past all the mess.
I know that He never fails us.
Though we fall short every day,
You've got to dust yourself off and go forward,
You've got to press on anyway.
For in the press lies your power.
In the press, there is faith.
In the press, there is joy.
In the press, there is grace.
In the press lies your healing.
In the press lies your strength.
So when you've finally surrendered,
That's when the press can move in.
For in the press is your blessing.
In the press is your purpose.
So lift your hands to the heavens,
And say, "God, let the press begin!"

She Played It Out (A Tribute to Maya Angelou)

Wise eyes whose journey goes beyond most human visibility and strength.
Writings that resonate in my heart of hurt, laughter,
Confidence and power to face unknown possibilities.
Possibilities.
All things are possible.
I can do all things.
She reminded many of the possibility.
Although Philippians 4:13 laid out the foundation over 2,000 years ago by the Promise Keeper,
She echoed the Promise beyond the wilderness to a people who lacked,
Lacked the ability to interpret the simple ink droplets on dirt-stained paper,
Which read, "Sign here."
She towered over many in stature and voice,
Yet she still had to "rise" in order to be heard
In a nation that deafened its ear to hear the screams in the

Ghettos of Harlem and the red-clay roads of Georgia.
Her lyrical dance and spoken-word crescendos, accompanied by pure southern slang,
Gave place and setting to a new representation in the high modernist era and days of the Harlem Renaissance Jazz movement.
God put the key in her hand, and she turned the lock.
"I'm out!" So glad to be me! So glad to be free!
Free to write it, speak it, name it, claim it, and rearrange it!
He laid it out for her to play it out,
And I am so happy to be a stage hand!
Encore! Encore!

Just Me! (Who Said That Wasn't Enough?)

I tried to be other things, but it was too much work. Too much work trying to be what the world thought I could be, should be, would have been, and could have been. I am me and if that's enough for God, it's enough for me.

Not mad about the people who say, "You are a pretty girl," but is that it? Really, is that all you see?

I am glad that God can see all of me--sweet, sassy, strong, classy, a thinker, a dreamer, an "out the box" go-getter in my own right. Can I get mad and angry please? Who do I need to ask can I get angry, cry, be hurt, and need to apologize?

Yeah, me! I owe apologies. How many? Too many to count. Who put me in this box, this box labeled, "Fragile, delicate, easily broken, light-weight, and batteries included?" I did not come with that stuff. I wasn't on sale or in the clearance aisle. So why do people over-talk me, like I am a given? Like the freebie on a test. Like the point you get for writing your name on the paper. I am me and if that's enough for God, it's enough for me. My silence is my thinking mode. Deal with it.

I don't like dresses. If I could wear them with gym shoes and mix-match socks, I would daily. Several times a day, I'd change them up, wash my face, and boom!

Make-up regiment is done, no special technique--water and soap, and wash it down the sink.

Aiming for that shine my daddy got back in 1986. Heard he got it from a Holy Ghost. Shoot, guess I wasn't ready for that at seven. I was still afraid of the dark. Ninety degrees outside, and I'm covered from head to toe in a blanket, sweating like I've been running in my sleep.

Alarm clock. Up. Okay, no socks. I overslept. High-tops on. No breakfast. No Sunday night press. Hair having a free day. Pass mom at the bus stop, holding our lunch so tight. Four-feet-eight taking care of ten-year-old, five-feet-two me. My lunch didn't feel so free, but she let me be me. And if that's enough for God, it's enough for me.

Preach, Daddy, preach! Teach, Daddy, teach! Love, Daddy, love! He needed love to learn *how* to love. God gave it to him and he prayed it through. I tarry, I tarry, even at the young age of ten years old. "Thank you, Jesus! Thank you, Jesus!" All night. You come back. No pants for me? No school dance for me? I don't know you, Daddy! You don't know me, Daddy! What's my favorite color? Favorite food, Daddy? I fell, Daddy. He broke my heart, Daddy! He made me cry, Daddy! I want to die, Daddy! How should he treat me, Daddy? Can you hear me, Daddy? No Daddy for me? God came, flipped the script, and gave it all to me. I flipped the script. The best gift you gave me? Your prayers were golden! Relationship restored! Thank God I am free! If that's enough for God, it's enough for me.

Five-feet-ten on the outside, inside feeling below an inch. Why make me so tall when all I wanted to do was to blend in? Not to be seen nor heard. Shhh. How will I learn? Oh no! Midnight! Now I can't speak.

Evil spirits visit me in my sleep. Tried to shut me out. I could not move, bandaged down by invisible struggles. They laughed at me, taunted me. I could not even cry. I could hear them just like when the kids on the street said I was too weak, and that God could not use me. I was too weak, never stood up for myself. I was too weak, couldn't speak. Had to pray in my mind, asking God to bind them up. Thank you, God, for being a mind regulator. Got my lesson, passed that test. No more evil spirits, no more mess! Got that Ghost. It helped me through the rest. I cannot hide, but the words will not come out. Wait! My lips are too small. Wait! The words cannot travel to be vocal at all.

Give no eye contact, give me long hair to hide. Ha! If I just stand very still, no one will notice me. Doing good…doing good… Oh no! I am clumsy. Tripping over everything.

Spill, drop, flop, kerplop! Man, I cannot win, but I am me. And if that's enough for God, it's enough for me.

Here they come! She is too tall, too skinny, big feet, four eyes, man hands, small lips, small nose, Dumbo ears, big head, and honky lover. Too nice, no back bone. Let a strong wind come. She too weak to stand strong. What happened? How could this be? What's all this mess, and is all this mess *me*?

Time gone good outweighing the bad. God forgave. Forgave. Forgave. Forgave. Forgave. Yeah, you get it.

Uh, oh! Phone call, It's Daddy:

"Hello. Okay, God? Oh, you said no more. You not taking this disobedience no more? Okay, Daddy. Too much? Okay. Grow up? Okay, no more pity parties. Okay, no more chicken Christian. Okay, Daddy. Do your will. No more trying to hide. Okay, no more fear and doubt. Okay, Daddy! Hell too hot, okay, Daddy! It won't work without you? Go back home? Okay, Daddy. It's what? Okay. 'It's all for my own good.' Okay, Daddy. Yes. I love you too."

When I Thought

When I thought you couldn't reach any deeper,
you reached down deeper, deeper.
When I thought you couldn't love me more, you
loved me more, much more.
When I thought you couldn't have more for me,
you delivered me completely.
When I thought you couldn't see me clearly, you
took fear from me, restored me wholly.
Just when my thoughts almost consumed me,
you took them over, gave new ones to me.
Now I can see you and stand here freely 'cause
in you, I have liberty.
When I thought there was no help for me, no
more mercy, grace wouldn't claim me.
Jesus, you showed there was more to you; I had
to die so your blood could run through.
It cleansed me completely, made this vessel
living and holy;
Acceptable to you to be used for your glory.
Now I stand here, knowing it was you, always
you.
So no matter what comes my way,
I can claim victory today.
You showed me what you put in me, and I won't
let no one set limits on my destiny.

I won't care how they look at me 'cause you love
me and know my story.
So just in case you don't know, I love you so
much,
Appreciate your touch.
And as I face tomorrow,
I hold my head up.
No more sorrow,
'Cause I know you live in me.
So I stand strong
In my victory.

Really

Traps are set daily to lure us in--
Traps of deceit and worldly pleasures that lead to sin.
This world can break you down
To the lowest common denominator,
Putting sin between you and the Creator,
Putting sin between you and the Throne.
Sin, we know, He can't
Look upon.
We all have a part to play.
If we confess His law,
We gotta kill this flesh every day--
Not just in front of those we "think" that count,
Because only God can get that clout.
So daily livin' on the top for Jesus
Is really what you gotta do.
The preacher, the teacher, yo mama, yo daddy, me and everybody else, too.

R.I.P. Flesh

That's how it had to be,
Either kill this flesh or kill what's in me.
This flesh was alive, but it wasn't living.
This vessel was moving, but it wasn't giving.
You can only kill something that's alive;
Don't let the enemy fool you with his disguise.
The stuff inside was full of self.
The use? What use? It was only good for looking at, nothing else.
You don't have to go to the movies to see The Walking Dead;
All you have to do is look at the world and the junk it's being fed.
All these so-called role models on videos and TV, with money and Ph.Ds.
Don't get caught up in the hype; it's poison disguised as sweet peas.
None of that will count, according to Revelation.
Money and education is an abomination without sanctification.
Have all that and lose my soul? For what?

Don't get caught up in American Idol; I want to make God's cut.
One table, three judges rolled into one, the Father, the Holy Ghost and the Son.
Do you; but do the "you" God made you to be.
Don't sell yourself short; go from glory to glory.
Level to level, movin' by mercy and grace,
Spreading His word, seeking His face.
Be all that you can be in the army of the Lord.
Seek Him first, and then claim His eternal reward.
Drop self in the garbage, with your pride and envy;
And any other trash that glorifies the enemy.
Do it quickly! Do not be fooled! The time grows near.
Not too long will the One and Only true God be here.
Don't you want to meet Him in the air?
I know I sho' nuff want to be there.

The Perfect Love Story

The perfect love story is not a cliché.
I live the perfect love story every day.
It cannot be found in man or vice;
It can only be found in Jesus Christ.
See, He died for me before I was born.
He knew that in this world, I would be scorned.
Shaken, abused, confused and hurt;
And, oh yes, even did my own dirt.
So He came down from Heaven to endure this world's strife,
And willingly gave up His life.
See the only perfect love story can come from Him.
Without His sacrifice, our after-life would be dim.
None of us are perfect, from the dainty to the hags.
The Word says on our best day, we are as filthy rags.
Perfect love story? The love of Christ!
Jesus over everything! Jesus for life!

See It Before You See It

You have to see it before you see it
Yeah, that's what I said.
Don't get it twisted or think God is playing with our heads.
"Now faith is…" says the Word, so you know it's true.
If God said it's yours, it shall be given to you.
For He is awesome, all powerful and never makes a mistake.
So sow the seed, which is the Word, and your harvest shall be great.
But don't look for it with the eyes of the flesh,
For by our spirit is how we get our best.
You have to see it before you see it;
Your faith has to shine!
Let God lead the way,
For He is holy and divine.
Don't worry about what's in your pocket or the bank.
Seek the Kingdom, keep your eye on the vision, pray and do not faint.
God hears you and will provide your every need.
Don't mess up and get that twisted with greed.
So see it before you see it. Then, it will be yours.
God will open up locked and chained doors!

Failure's Not an Option

Failure's not an option, so stop giving it space.
Got the world on top when that's God's place.
Don't look at me funny like you don't know;
Just reminding you of what God told you a long time ago.
Do you know me? My character and where I've been?
If so, you know God anointed this pen.
I am only a vessel, used to write what He tells me to.
Gotta wait for His direction so the words will be true.
So check mark on that; let's get back to the lesson.
Don't want you to miss out on your blessin'.
Failure's not an option, not a choice at all.
Stop placing your hope in the world's four walls.
You gotta step out to step into your destiny.
As God ministers to you, He ministers to me.
Follow God's commandments and He'll take care of the rest.
You may be under some pressure, but never claim stress.
You may be concerned; but worrying, we don't do.
Watch what you claim to be in 'cause failure's not an option for you.
So speak life to all that is good, and God will provide like He said He would.
Don't believe me? All I can do is try.
But God said, "He will," and He is not a man that He should lie.

Letter (or Notice) to the Devil

You think you got me?
Don't be fooled.
My Father walks in the cool.
You think you got me?
My mind going around.
You think you slick,
Like you got me pinned down?
Don't think my storm will get you peace,
That this trial I'm in will be your increase.
You can't have free range in my body, you see,
Cause God is close and in me.
You trying to play with my mind.
God, these thoughts trying to take me over all the time.
Thoughts of lust, lies and deceit,
Trying to make me think that you, I can't defeat?
Want to use me to do your dirt?
Back up off; I'm raining peace.
You gon' get yo feelings hurt.
Want to use me to think my Holy Ghost ain't real,
Trying to stop my growth in my purpose that I must fulfill.

Want me to stay weak and not use the power God gave me,
When I know that He called me out and saved me.
I refuse to bow down; I will fight to the end,
Cause I know, on God, I can depend.
So while you keep playing games, tryin' to get me to be that girl you once knew,
I just want to say, "I'm so over you!"

Stop Being So Selfish

Stop being so selfish with your gift for real;
Got it all wrapped up with a zip-lock seal.
It's not yours anyway.
God gave it to you to help someone along the way.
You think you're special. Okay, let's see.
Stop balling up and crumbling, like the dead root of a tree.
You better be careful, cause you on a thin line.
Put your gift to use cause you running out of time.
No, I'm not trying to judge or fuss at you.
This message is for me, too.
God deals with us all on getting this done,
Reminding us that our freedom was paid for by His Son.
So we must use what He gave us, before it's too late.
For we know not the year, month or date.
We want to be caught doing His will,
Not doing what the world does still.
So get busy in doing what God has called you to do.
Time and life will not stand still for your slothfulness to continue.
I'm not telling you what I heard; this is what I know.
God dealt with me and continues to show,
That I must stay on track.
The price is too high.
I don't want to leave here in sin,

Because in them, I will die.
But this is not how it has to be, for in Christ, is victory and liberty.

Don't Stop Praying

Don't stop praying.
If you do, you're delaying
Your own breakthrough.
Don't let the enemy confuse you.
Pray without ceasing;
Watch your power start increasing.
Make that worship come from the depth of your soul.
Rebuke that enemy; bind every stronghold.
Step on Satan's face; spit in his eye.
He could care less about you and I.
He wants you to be quiet and keep your lips tight,
To stay in darkness, not come into the marvelous light.
He comes to kill, steal and destroy us all.
You making his job easy if you leanin' on the world's walls.
You can't stumble if you're on your knees.
So drop down and give God 10 "Hallelujahs!" please!

Pounding Heart

Here I am, Lord; this is it.
I need to be held and told it will be okay.
Tears I cry through the night and part of the day.
What happened to how I thought it would be?
Who came and ripped my life's dreams from me?
Why does growing have to hurt so much?
All I wanted was comfort; every now and then, a touch.
Father, this is your daughter.
You know my day-to-day cry.
I work hard at being pleasing in your eyes.
I only want to live right so I can see you one day,
So you can reach deep and take all my hurt and pain away.
Keep me safe, Lord. I was hurt so bad.
Dreams were shattered. No mom, no dad.
Why did he try to take my spirit?
Try to disgrace and kill what you put in it?
So selfish, sold for things.
Laid my feelings and pain aside, like they were nothing.
Shut down. Felt worthless, so I sought out affection.
From man to boy to man, trying to make a connection.
It was the most vulnerable part of her life that she felt strife.
Wanted to jump to take her own life.

But she knew one day, someone would need this testimony.
That it was not you, Lord, that let this happen, you see.
But she got through it, like she knew she would.
What the devil meant for evil, God used it for good.

The Main Thing

What's the main thing?
Can you look and guess?
Try to use the world to answer your best?
Is the main thing money?
We need it. True.
Is it material things? Has the answer come to you?
The main thing, the most important...
Number 1 on the list?
Question got your eyes lookin' up and your mouth in a twist?
Where do you start to look?
Need a clue, some hint?
Okay, a book.
Not *a* book, but *the* Book, and every word in it.
The book is not for sale, and it's free what's in it.
It's the Bible--the true and infallible written Word of God.
Come on really? Was it that hard?
The main thing...what's the main thing?
The Word of God takes the spot.
It teaches us what's right and wrong.
Do you read it, eat it, and live it every day?
Do you use it for direction, meditate on it when you pray?
If not, stop reading these words right away.
Get into the Word that will keep you righteous day by day.

Beauty

Man measures beauty by what he sees with his eyes;
The perfect smile and bright eyes;
Slender shape and thick thighs;
Curvy hips and round backside.
But what about crooked smiles and lazy eyes?
Full shapes, flat back side and no thighs?
Could the outside be hiding something deeper on the inside?
A hard heart, with soft lips.
A liar or thief with smooth finger tips.
Mean and vicious with a laugh so sweet;
Walks with grace, quick on hustle feet.
Spitting venom and words of love with the same tongue;
Wishing someone well and waiting for their bottom to fall out and watch them Get hung.
Can this be controlled? Who passes the test?
Those who humble themselves, knowing neither is better or less.
Only God's measurements count in the end.

Take a look,
Beauty on the outside will not get you an ink drop in the Book.
What book? No self, *Ebony* or *Jet*.
But the Book of Life, and that's no joke.
To get my name in, I will go for broke!

Say Whaaat?

Tongue got you in trouble again?
Too many words can lead you to sin.
Sometimes, what you let out your throat,
Can damage the integrity of some folk.
Keep busy and give your problems to God alone.
He will listen and teach you how to fix your wrong.
What you let out that mouth, you can't subtract.
But He will cover you, when you are sincere, when others try to attack.
He forgets your sins when you ask for forgiveness with sincerity and truth.
He prepares your heart for the correction and reproof.
So if you said it, repent, forgive yourself and move on.
Let God clean the dirt out your mouth because then, it's surely gone.

You See

The game doesn't change, only the players.
Gotta clean your spirit daily;
Peel off the dirty layers.
The devil will use whoever he can--
Boy, girl, man or woman--ain't no limits to his dirty hands.
Keep your mind stayed on the Lord and He will renew your strength.
Don't be swayed or confused like the Church of Corinth.
Know now that God has your back.
When you let Him live in you, you will never lack.
Only with Him, can you be your best.
Even at your best, remember you're still a hot mess.
Therefore, we gotta get clean every day.
Ask God to keep all that sin away.
See, sin is not just what you do; it's what you think, feel and say, too.
The tongue is like a two-edged sword.
Gotta keep it from slippin' so you can see your reward.
Don't even think about that if you're not seeking Him first.
Matthew 6:33 doesn't work in reverse.
So press toward the mark and stay in the race.
If you fall, get up; wipe the dirt off your face.
Don't stay down there and start crawlin';
God is more than well able to keep you from fallin'.

What's Next?

So, ya saved! Got that sin out your life.
Rid yourself of all that mess and strife.
Okay.
Came.
Saved.
Step three is next to do.
Let the Holy Ghost come upon you.
Don't live beneath your privilege, my friend.
Get full, then you get power that will live within.
Superman cannot compete with this power and might,
That reaches beyond this world's imagination and laughs at kryptonite.
It gives you the ability to stand on the Word, in the Word and for the Word.
To go against the grain and norm;
To give it all to Jesus and not conform.

Devil, You Make Me Sick!

I AM SO SICK AND TIRED OF YOU!
SOON AS I SAY WE ARE THROUGH,
HERE YOU GO CALLING ME IN THE MIDDLE OF
THE NIGHT,
TRYING TO GET ME TO DO WRONG, WHEN
YOU KNOW I'M TRYING TO LIVE RIGHT.
ALWAYS TRYIN' TO BE IN MY EAR AND TELL ME
WHAT TO SAY.
HUSH YOUR MOUTH! GET OUT MY FACE!
I DON'T HAVE TIME FOR YOU TOMORROW OR
ANY OTHER DAY.
MY DADDY SAID, "KEEP AWAY FROM HERE NOW;
LEAVE MY DAUGHTER ALONE!"
PACK YOUR LUST, ENVY AND JEALOUSY, AND
GO BACK TO HELL WHERE YOU BELONG!
DON'T TURN BACK! OH, YOU FORGOT
SOMETHING?
YOUR DISEASE AND HATRED, TOO?
DON'T WORRY. IN JESUS' NAME, WE WILL
REBUKE IT TO YOU!

Get the Truth

Get the truth;
Don't settle for less.
Get the truth;
God wants to give you His best.
Get the truth;
You ain't got much time.
Get the truth;
Don't let Satan take over ya mind.
Get the truth;
It's not a game.
Get the truth;
Cause you want Him to know your name.
Get the truth;
The choice is yours.
Get the truth;
God's not gonna bust down the doors.
Get the truth;
He is gentle and sweet.
And only in Him, are you complete.
Get the truth;
Get ya nose out the air.
Get the truth;
Hell is hot and it's real, oh yeah!
Get the truth;
You're not too young to go.
Get the truth;
Satan will welcome you with open arms,

fa sho!
Get the truth;
Don't give in.
Get the truth;
This world? It's not your friend!
Get the truth!

Just My Rant

Don't quiet me! I have something to say.
Ahhhh! But I'm waiting for God to tell me that it's okay.
He said, "Yes," so here it is.
God says, "Get over yourself and leave it alone."
Leave what?
Whatever got you livin' wrong.
I don't know about you, but I refuse to go to hell
I don't like it over 78 degrees outside. (I'm just sayin').

Pray for My Generation

Can you pray for my generation?
They don't know the deal.
They keep selling crack, when they know it kills.
Can you pray for my generation?
They are wasting time.
Can't study for a test, but can spill lyrics and create 20-minute rap lines.
Can you pray for my generation?
Trying to grow up too fast.
Not wanting responsibility of a grown-up, but wanting the freedom and cash.
Can you pray for my generation?
Clear away the smoke.
Before this world consumes them and in their sins, they choke.
Can you pray for my generation?
All caught up in self.
Tell them not to sell out, but *be* sold out,
Cause God is present help.
Can you pray for my generation?
That they don't take the blame.
Just because momma and daddy did it, they don't have to inherit the shame.
Can you pray for my generation?
As they go day by day, trying to figure out why they are here anyway.

Can you pray for my generation?
Trying to fill their hearts' void with sex, money, drugs and everything else;
Not knowing God left that spot only for Himself.
Can we pray for our generation?
My teen years have passed.
But what I asked you to pray for still needs to be asked.

I'm Already Convinced

See my feelings got me feeling myself.
If I'm feeling myself, I'm not feeling your help.
There's a war going on between my spirit and my flesh.
To let my thoughts consume me gives flesh the championship belt.
So Lord, let your spirit overtake me; let me hide in you.
This world out here is trying to strangle the truth;
Trying to choke out your Word and devalue your name;
Twisting scripture, the meaning, and shouting believers
Are to blame.
Building walls of hate to divide us even more;
It would be too much like right for us to walk
On one accord.
The game hasn't changed, only the players.
Gotta clean this flesh daily; peel off the dirty layers.
We can't compromise the promise or waiver in our faith.
These Facebook statuses keep screaming
Unforgiveness, hurt, hate and love misplaced.
This should keep us on our face.
It's like the Israelites crying out for relief and a
Savior to appear,

Not realizing their liberation and care package was already here!
It's not FEMA, the government or new car for everyone!
It's the blood of Jesus Christ,
Who's kept it real since day one.
Not sharing to convince you, but because I'm already convinced,
I've been commissioned to spread the Word. Does that make any sense?
It's like a teacher who is passionate to share what they know,
Or a kid eagerly waiting to shine at a talent show.
Like a blossomed butterfly who had a hole in its cocoon,
By His stripes, they were healed, and had no trace of a wound.
So to wrap up this verse that could preach on its own,
I really didn't need all these words because God's Word is good enough on its own.
But because lyrical soliloquies with a blank verse or rhyme,
Seem to pause a thought of reflection on the mind.
God gifted me to type and right click this, so boom!
God bless you, and consider yourself ministered to.

About the Author

Kayvonna K. Stigall is a native of River Rouge, Michigan. She is married and has two children. She is a teacher, poet and author and believes wholeheartedly that writing is what God has called her to do. Writing and sharing her writings with the world is her passion and she hopes it will inspire others to rise above their situation; no matter what chaos or distractions may be in their way. *The Rise Above the Clouds* is not only the title of her book but it is also the name of her business. Kayvonna conducts poetry workshops and classes during the summer for school districts in the Metro-Detroit area as well as summer camps. In addition, she writes poetry for special occasions and participates in spoken word events. Look out for her second collection of poetry in the fall of 2016.

For more information contact her at:
riseabovetheclouds5@gmail.com

www.ingramcontent.com/pod-product-compliance
Lightning Source LLC
Chambersburg PA
CBHW021159080526
44588CB00008B/417